Explore the Universe

THE UNIVERSE—
A COSMIC TOUR

WORLD
BOOK

a Scott Fetzer company
Chicago
www.worldbookonline.com

World Book, Inc.
233 N. Michigan Avenue
Chicago, IL 60601
U.S.A.

For information about other World Book publications, visit our
Web site at **http://www.worldbookonline.com** or call
1-800-WORLDBK (967-5325).

For information about sales to schools and
libraries, call **1-800-975-3250 (United States)**,
or **1-800-837-5365 (Canada)**.

Library of Congress Cataloging-in-Publication data
The universe—a cosmic tour.
    p. cm. -- (Explore the universe)
    Summary: "An overview of the structure and nature of objects
that make up the universe. Includes diagrams, fun facts,
glossary, resource list, and index"--Provided by publisher.
    Includes index.
    ISBN 978-0-7166-9545-5
    1. Cosmology--Juvenile literature. 2. Astrophysics--
Juvenile literature. I. World Book, Inc.
    QB983.U555 2010
    523--dc22
                                    2009042609

ISBN 978-0-7166-9544-8 (set)
Printed in China at Leo Paper Products, LTD.,
    Heshan, Guangdong
1st printing February 2010

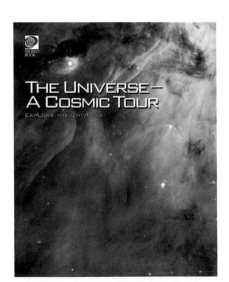

Cover image:
Untold numbers of bright
new stars forming in the
Orion Nebula glitter among
swirling clouds of dust and
gas in a stunning, false-color
image from the Hubble Space
Telescope.

NASA, ESA, and The Hubble
Heritage Team (STScI/AURA)

CONTENTS

If a word is printed in **bold letters that look like this,** that word's meaning is given in the glossary on pages 60-61.

INTRODUCTION

The universe was created in an instant, according to strong scientific evidence. All of the matter that makes up all of the objects in the universe was compacted into a space smaller than an atom. In the blink of an eye, the universe expanded from this tiny point to the size of an entire galaxy. It continues to expand today. As the universe grew, matter changed from the exotic and mysterious to the more familiar. It collected together to form galaxies, stars, and planets. Eventually, some matter on Earth became animals, plants, and human beings.

Our universe is everything that exists around us. It may also be everything that has or will exist in time and space. But our universe may not be all there is. It is possible that other universes have existed in the past. It is possible that other universes exist now.

The Carina Nebula, one of the brightest regions of the Milky Way Galaxy, is also one of the galaxy's largest star-forming regions. Forty-eight images from the Hubble Space Telescope were combined to create the colorized, panoramic view. ▶

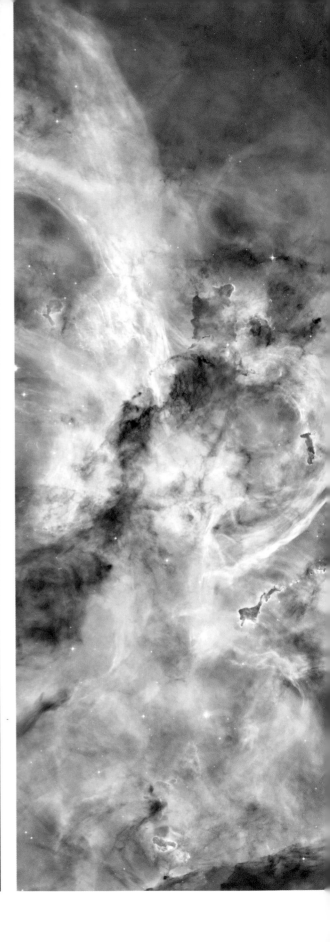

The universe is everything around us. It is everything that we see when we look up into the sky. It includes the sun, moon, and **stars.** It includes Earth, all the **planets,** and every other object in the **solar system** as well as everything farther out in space.

Clouds of gas cast off by a dying star erupt into space at more than 600,000 miles (966,000 kilometers) per hour, in a false-color image made by the Hubble Space Telescope. The shrinking core of the star, once similar in size to our sun, will become a glowing, Earth-sized object called a white dwarf.

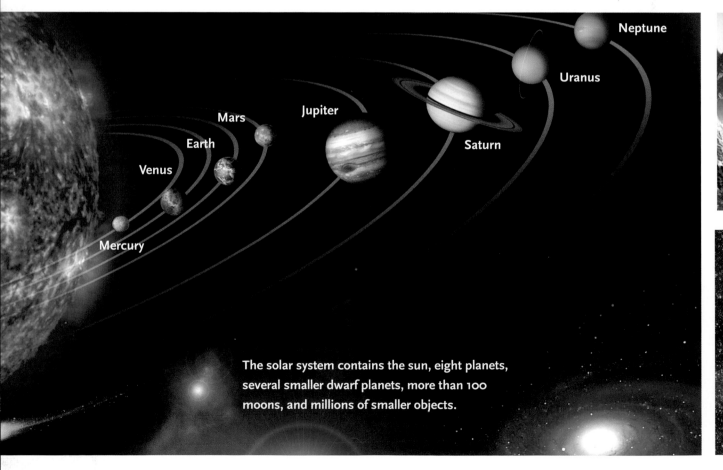

Neptune

Uranus

Jupiter

Mars

Earth

Saturn

Venus

Mercury

The solar system contains the sun, eight planets, several smaller dwarf planets, more than 100 moons, and millions of smaller objects.

The universe is everything that exists anywhere in space and time.

THINGS SEEN AND UNSEEN

There is much more to the universe than the things we can see. Powerful telescopes show astronomers that the universe stretches for incredible distances. It holds stars, **galaxies,** and such strange objects as gravity-monster **black holes** and **quasars,** some of the brightest objects in the universe. In addition, most of the matter in the universe seems to be invisible to the scientific instruments we use today.

STUDIES AND THEORIES

Astronomers who study the development of the universe are called **cosmologists.** They try to discover how big and how old the universe is. They study the structure of the universe and the forces that shape it. They develop theories about how the universe began—and how it might end. Cosmologists often work with physicists who study matter and energy. The science of applying the rules of physics to the study of the universe is called astrophysics.

Water and other potentially life-forming chemicals pool around rocks on an imaginary extrasolar planet in an artist's illustration. The planet is shown orbiting a red dwarf, a star cooler than the sun.

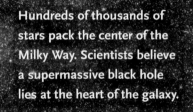

Hundreds of thousands of stars pack the center of the Milky Way. Scientists believe a supermassive black hole lies at the heart of the galaxy.

The universe might be shaped like a sphere, or ball. It might be shaped like a donut. The universe that astronomers can observe appears to be flat. The universe, however, might not have any edge that would give it a shape because it might go on forever.

The universe is so big that it is difficult to even imagine the distances involved. The distances from one **star** or **galaxy** to another are so vast that astronomers have devised special ways of measuring them.

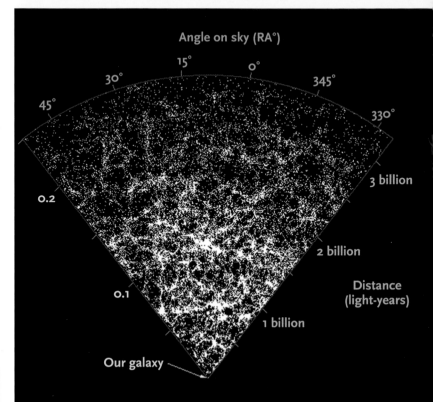

Angle on sky (RA°)

15°
30°
0°
45°
345°
330°
0.2
3 billion
2 billion
0.1
Distance (light-years)
1 billion
Our galaxy

A map showing the locations of 52,000 galaxies in one section of the universe clearly reveals how galaxies clump together to form filaments. The galaxies closer to us seem to clump together tightly, and galaxies farther away seem to be more spread out.

Early observations of the universe suggested it could be one of several shapes. Satellite measurements in the 2000's have shown the universe is virtually flat, like a piece of paper.

DID YOU KNOW?

Astronomers call the area of the universe beyond the center of the Milky Way the "zone of avoidance" because gas and dust in our galaxy block out visible light coming from objects there.

No one knows the size or shape of the universe. However, recent measurements taken by a probe indicate it may be close to flat.

LIGHT-YEARS

One of the basic units of distance that astronomers use is the light-year. This is the distance that a pulse of light travels through a vacuum in one year. Light travels at 186,282 miles (299,792 kilometers) per second. Therefore, a pulse of light can cover about 5.88 trillion miles (9.46 trillion kilometers) in one year.

MOST DISTANT OBJECTS

The most distant object found as of 2009 was an exploding **star** whose light took 13.1 billion years to reach Earth. The exploding star gave off a tremendous burst of high-energy rays called **gamma rays.** Astronomers first detected the star with an instrument that "sees" gamma rays. They then pointed other telescopes at the gamma-ray burst. These other telescopes measure **_infrared_** (heat) radiation. Astronomers use infrared light to detect how far away an object is in the universe.

Astronomers can see only as far away—and as far back in time—as their best telescopes will allow. As astronomers develop ever more-powerful telescopes and other instruments, they will be able to detect objects that are even farther away.

Some of the oldest galaxies in the universe shine brightly in an image called the Hubble Deep Field, taken by the Hubble Space Telescope in 1995. Light from these galaxies traveled from 5 billion to 10 billion years to get to Earth. To create this long look into the past, the Hubble viewed a single portion of the sky for 10 days.

ANALYZING LIGHT

Visible light consists of all the colors of the rainbow, from violet and blue to orange and red. But it is just a small part of a larger "rainbow" of energy called the electromagnetic spectrum. The spectrum goes from low-energy radio waves at one end to high-energy X rays and gamma rays at the other.

Visible light and all other types of electromagnetic energy travel across space as waves. Different kinds of electromagnetic energy have different wavelengths. Wavelength is the distance from the *crest* (top) of one wave to another. Shorter waves have more energy than longer waves.

Astronomers use instruments called spectroscopes or spectrometers to examine light from objects in space. These instruments spread out wavelengths of light into a rainbow-like pattern called a spectrum. The chemical elements in stars, galaxies, and other objects make bright or dark lines in a spectrum. Every object has a different spectrum based on the different chemical elements from which it is made.

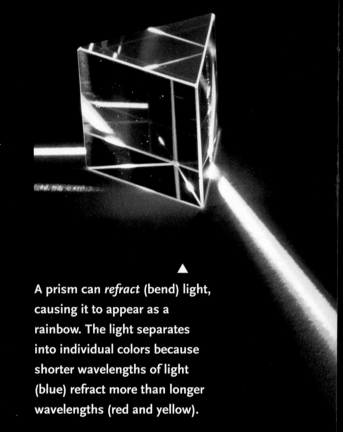

▲
A prism can *refract* (bend) light, causing it to appear as a rainbow. The light separates into individual colors because shorter wavelengths of light (blue) refract more than longer wavelengths (red and yellow).

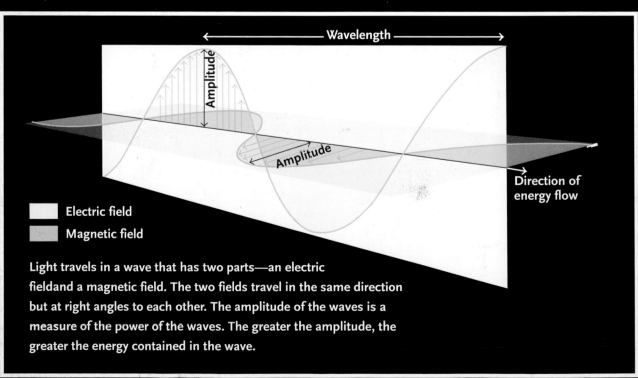

Electric field
Magnetic field

Light travels in a wave that has two parts—an electric fieldand a magnetic field. The two fields travel in the same direction but at right angles to each other. The amplitude of the waves is a measure of the power of the waves. The greater the amplitude, the greater the energy contained in the wave.

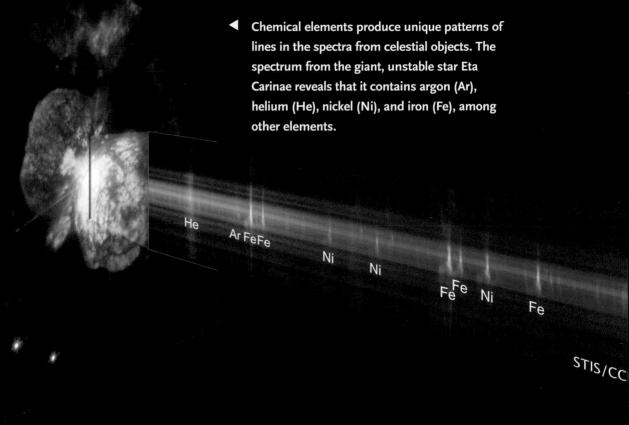

Chemical elements produce unique patterns of lines in the spectra from celestial objects. The spectrum from the giant, unstable star Eta Carinae reveals that it contains argon (Ar), helium (He), nickel (Ni), and iron (Fe), among other elements.

He   Ar FeFe   Ni   Ni   Fe   Fe Ni   Fe

STIS/CC

WFPC2

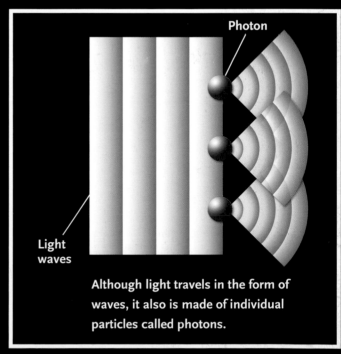

Photon

Light waves

Although light travels in the form of waves, it also is made of individual particles called photons.

MOVING TOWARD THE RED

The lines in the **spectrum** of light coming from an object usually appear in a particular **wavelength.** Much of the light that we observe shows **redshift,** or a shift toward longer, redder wavelengths and away from the shorter, bluer end of the spectrum. Wavelengths can be shortened or lengthened depending on whether an object is moving toward or away from Earth. When an object is moving toward Earth, its light waves are pressed together and so become shorter. When an object is moving away, its light waves are stretched and so become longer.

There are two main causes of redshift. The first is caused by the **Doppler effect**. This is the same effect that causes a train whistle to have a higher pitch when the train is moving toward you and a lower pitch when the train is moving away.

The second cause of redshift is cosmological redshift. This shift is not caused by the movement of **stars** but by the expansion of space itself. When astronomers discuss redshift, they are usually referring to cosmological redshift.

Scientists believe that the universe began about 13.7 billion years ago in an explosion called the **big bang.** Since then, the universe has expanded from a single point to its present size. As the universe expands, it stretches light traveling through space, much as a spring is stretched as its ends are pulled apart.

Astronomers can learn about a star's motion by analyzing the light it gives off. If a star's light is shifted toward the red end of the spectrum, the star is moving away from Earth. If the light is shifted toward the blue end of the spectrum, the star is moving toward us.

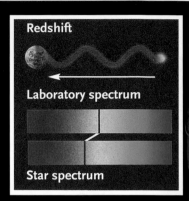

Redshift

Laboratory spectrum

Star spectrum

Scientists believe that after the big bang, the universe immediately began to expand. The distances between stars, galaxies, and other objects grew as space expanded. Scientists can measure the expansion of space by observing the effect it has on light waves. As space expands, it stretches the light traveling through it. By measuring the amount of stretching—called redshift—scientists can estimate the rate of expansion.

The big bang

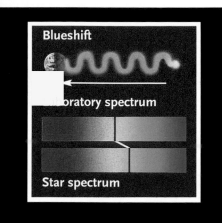

Blueshift

Laboratory spectrum

Star spectrum

The farther light has traveled, the more cosmological redshift it shows. Light from the most distant **galaxies** shows the strongest redshift. Such light has been stretched so much that it arrives as **infrared** or **radio waves.** By measuring redshift, astronomers can measure the distance to faraway galaxies. They can also determine an object's speed. The faster an object is moving in relation to Earth, the more the light is redshifted.

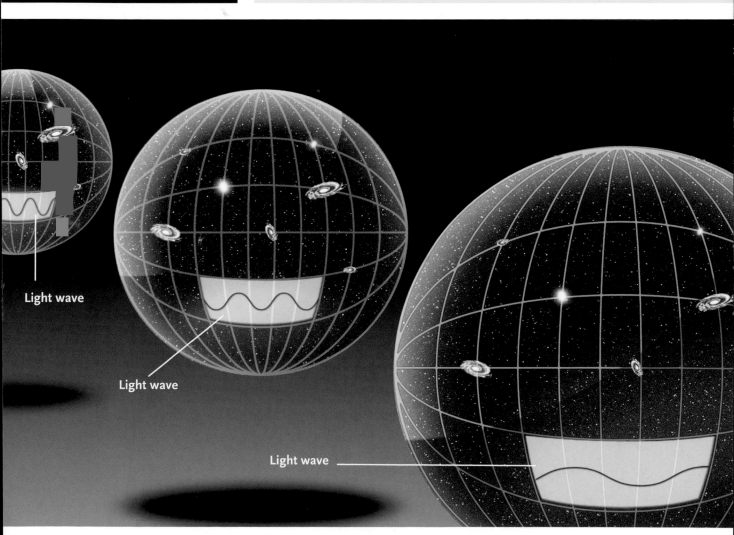

Light wave

Light wave

Light wave

RAPID INFLATION

A theory called **inflation theory** explains what happened right after the **big bang.** According to inflation theory, the universe expanded very rapidly in the first few seconds. Imagine the early universe as a balloon. Suppose you attach the balloon to a tank of gas and open the nozzle all the way. The balloon will inflate, or blow up, very quickly. According to inflation theory, the universe grew from less than the size of a pinpoint to the size of a **galaxy** in just a fraction of a second. Inflation stopped when the universe cooled down and matter as we know it began to form.

A theory sometimes known as "the big bounce" suggests that the universe expands and contracts in a repeating cycle. According to this theory, a universe similar to ours existed before the big bang. After a period of expansion, that previous universe began to shrink. When it shrank to a point smaller than an atom, it exploded into the current universe in the big bang.

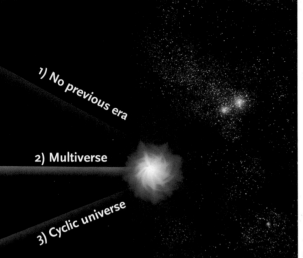

1) No previous era

2) Multiverse

3) Cyclic universe

Most scientists agree that the big bang marked the beginning of the current universe. However, there is no current way to observe events before this event. Scientists have theorized: (1) that nothing may have existed before the big bang; (2) that there may be many possible universes and that the big bang occurred when two of them touched; (3) that our current universe may be just one in a repeating cycle of expansion, contraction, and big bangs.

TINY FIREBALL

It is hard to imagine what things were like at the moment of the **big bang.** For the tiniest fraction of a second, the entire universe was unimaginably hot and dense. Some scientists describe the universe of this time as a tiny, primordial fireball. It was thousands of times smaller than the head of a pin. Space and time as we think of them did not even exist.

Previous universe

an event that they call the big bang.

STILL EXPANDING

Astronomers have found that the universe is still expanding. They see galaxies moving farther away from Earth as well as from one another. **Cosmologists** say the galaxies appear to be moving because space itself is continuing to expand.

The current universe

e big
g

Some scientists theorize that the universe we live in exists on a membrane-like surface called a brane, or a "braneworld" (below). This brane is only a thin slice of the entire "megaverse," which consists of extra dimensions we cannot detect. According to this idea, other universes on other branes also make thin slices through the multidimensional megaverse.

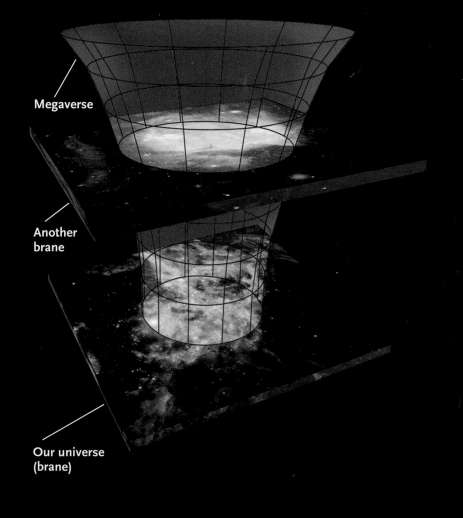

Megaverse

Another brane

Our universe (brane)

Estimating the age of the universe calls for some clever detective work. **Cosmologists** check for clues in two main areas. They look for the oldest **stars,** because the universe cannot be younger than the oldest stars. They also try to figure out how rapidly the universe is expanding.

LOOKING FOR OLD STARS

Cosmologists use large groupings of stars, called **globular clusters,** as gigantic "clocks." Some globular clusters contain several million stars held close together by the force of **gravity.** All of the stars in any particular globular cluster appear to have formed at about the same time. They also formed long ago. These stars contain mainly **hydrogen** and **helium,** the first **chemical elements** to form. With very few exceptions, they do not contain heavier elements, which formed later from exploding stars.

Stars, however, are different sizes. The bigger and brighter a star, the faster it will use up its fuel and die. Astronomers know the rate at which stars of different sizes use fuel. They estimate that the oldest stars are between 11 billion and 13 billion years old.

RATE OF EXPANSION

Astronomers try to estimate the age of the universe using a mathematical formula. To make the formula work, they need to know

Globular clusters, such as NGC 6093 (center), serve as "clocks" to help scientists measure the age of the universe because their stars are extremely old and formed at about the same time.

Cosmologists estimate that the universe is about 13.7 billion years old.

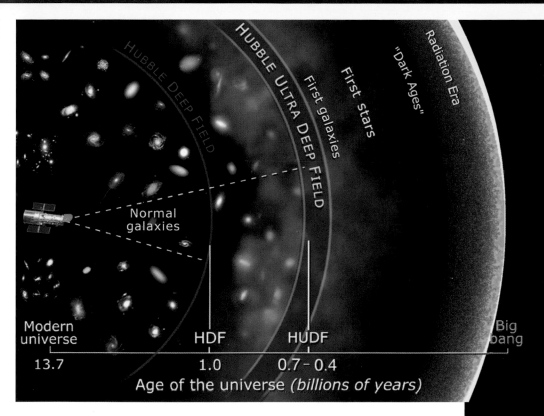

HUBBLE DEEP FIELD

HUBBLE ULTRA DEEP FIELD

First galaxies

First stars

"Dark Ages"

Radiation Era

Normal galaxies

Modern universe	HDF	HUDF	Big bang
13.7	1.0	0.7 - 0.4	

Age of the universe *(billions of years)*

how rapidly the universe is expanding now. Measurements of the expansion taken with the orbiting Wilkinson Microwave Anisotropy Probe (WMAP) helped them make better estimates. Cosmologists now estimate the age of the universe as 13.7 billion years.

There is also a connection between age and distance. It takes light from a distant object a certain amount of time to reach Earth. So, the farther out in space you look, the further back you look in time. Light from the most distant **galaxies** we can observe has traveled for about 13 billion years. These objects formed soon after the **big bang.**

Two studies conducted by the Hubble Space Telescope have obtained views of the universe as it appeared more than 13 billion years ago. The Hubble Deep Field shows galaxies as they appeared 12.7 billion years ago, only 1 billion years after the big bang. The Hubble Ultra Deep Field shows galaxies that formed about 500 million years after the big bang. These galaxies are near the edge of what astronomers call the observable universe, the part of the universe that we can see.

HOW MATTER FORMED IN THE EARLY UNIVERSE

Scientific evidence strongly suggests that the universe began in a cosmic event called the big bang. This event is said to have created the universe and all the matter in it. In the very first microseconds after the big bang, the universe was a mixture of matter, antimatter, and energy. When matter and antimatter come into contact with each other, both are destroyed, leaving behind only energy. However, for reasons not yet known, the early universe came into being with slightly more matter than antimatter. The destruction of nearly all antimatter left only energy and a "small" amount of matter. This excess matter went on to form atoms and, eventually, stars, galaxies, planets and every other object in the universe.

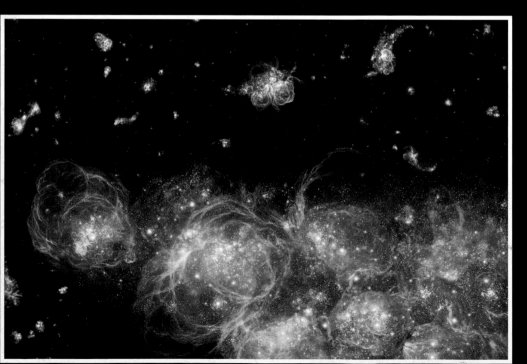

Thousands of stars burst into existence in the early universe like fireworks exploding during a grand finale, in an artist's illustration. The first stars may have formed in huge numbers over a short period, according to findings made using the Hubble Space Telescope.

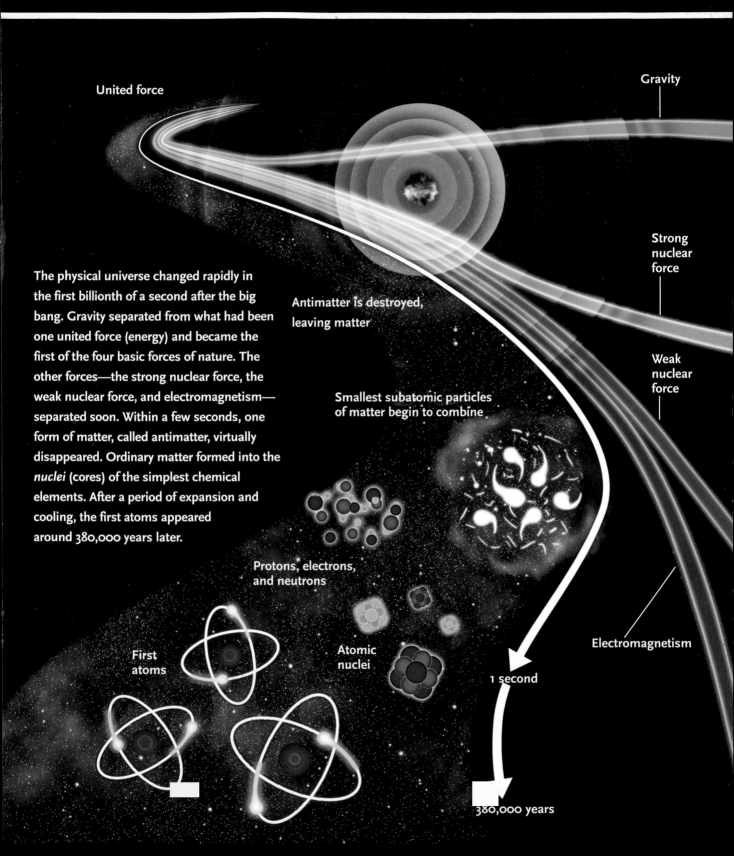

United force

Gravity

Strong
nuclear
force

Weak
nuclear
force

Electromagnetism

The physical universe changed rapidly in the first billionth of a second after the big bang. Gravity separated from what had been one united force (energy) and became the first of the four basic forces of nature. The other forces—the strong nuclear force, the weak nuclear force, and electromagnetism—separated soon. Within a few seconds, one form of matter, called antimatter, virtually disappeared. Ordinary matter formed into the *nuclei* (cores) of the simplest chemical elements. After a period of expansion and cooling, the first atoms appeared around 380,000 years later.

Antimatter is destroyed, leaving matter

Smallest subatomic particles of matter begin to combine

Protons, electrons, and neutrons

First atoms

Atomic nuclei

1 second

380,000 years

WHAT IS THE COSMIC MICROWAVE BACKGROUND RADIATION?

A LUCKY ACCIDENT

The **CMB** radiation was first predicted in the 1940's, though it was not detected until the 1960's. American physicists Arno Penzias and Robert W. Wilson discovered the CMB radiation by accident. The physicists were using a **microwave** observatory at Bell Laboratories in New Jersey to study gas surrounding the Milky Way. But they ran into a problem. The observatory picked up unwanted microwave radiation "noise." The microwaves were not coming from the gas. They were coming from every direction in the universe. The physicists concluded that the microwaves were radiation left over from the **big bang**. For providing this strong evidence to support the big bang theory, Penzias and Wilson shared in the 1978 Nobel Prize in physics.

Scientists believe that the early universe was filled with high-energy **electromagnetic radiation,** including **gamma rays** and **X rays.** As the universe expanded and cooled, about 380,000 years after the big bang, the radiation took on less energetic forms, including **visible** and **infrared light.** Over time, the radiation continued to cool. Today, we see it as microwave radiation.

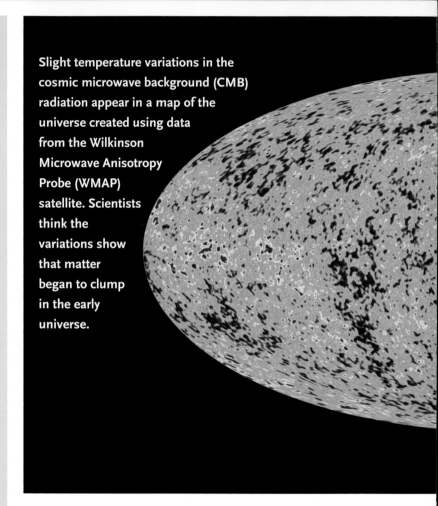

Slight temperature variations in the cosmic microwave background (CMB) radiation appear in a map of the universe created using data from the Wilkinson Microwave Anisotropy Probe (WMAP) satellite. Scientists think the variations show that matter began to clump in the early universe.

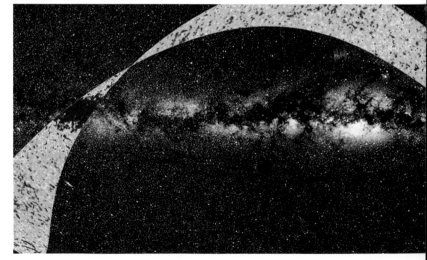

The cosmic microwave background (CMB) radiation is a faint glow of energy left over from the birth of the universe.

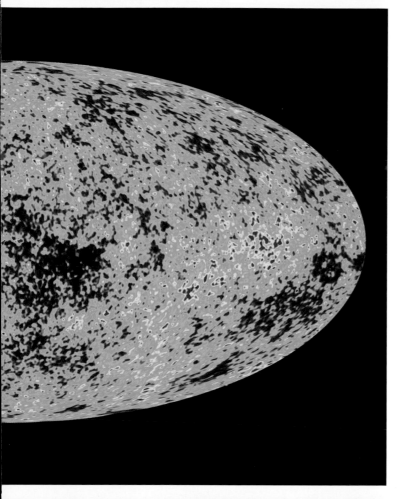

THE CLUMPING OF MATTER

Research satellites have helped scientists learn more about the CMB radiation. The Cosmic Background Explorer (COBE), launched in 1989, took the temperature of the background radiation. COBE found slight differences in the temperatures from different directions. Cooler areas are believed to represent areas of greater density. Another satellite, the Wilkinson Microwave Anisotropy Probe (WMAP), launched in 2001, continued to observe and map these variations. Scientists believe the findings show that as the early universe cooled, matter began to form clumps. Billions of years later, the clumping of matter had led to the formation of galaxies seen today. In 2009, the Planck observatory was launched with the hope of getting the most detailed map of the CMB radiation ever recorded.

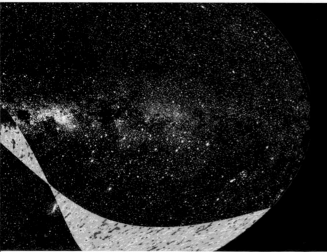

One of the first images of the CMB radiation from the Planck observatory, superimposed on a photograph of the Milky Way, is nearly as detailed as images gathered by the WMAP project over five years. Planck images are expected to become even more detailed as the probe continues to scan the CMB radiation. (Red sections in the image represent interference from the Milky Way.)

WHAT IS MATTER?

Scientists think that all the matter in **planets,** plants, people, and everything else in the universe was born in events that began more than 13 billion years ago, when space and time began with the **big bang.**

BUILDING BLOCKS OF MATTER

The matter that formed in the first few seconds after the big bang was very strange stuff. It was an intensely hot "soup" of the basic building blocks of the universe.

Some of the first known particles of matter were **quarks.** Quarks are elementary particles—that is, they appear to have no smaller parts. In fact, they are so small that there is no way to measure them. As the universe grew cooler and bigger, quarks joined together to make larger particles called *protons* (positively charged particles) and *neutrons* (particles with no electric charge). The quarks in protons and neutrons are held together with particles called gluons.

Within the first three minutes after the big bang, the temperature of the universe had dropped to less

The surface of the sun is a violent mass of hot gas and a gas-like form of matter called plasma.

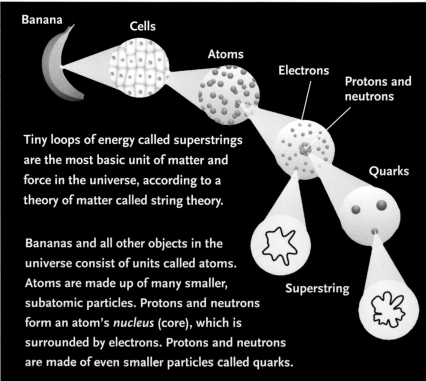

Banana Cells Atoms Electrons Protons and neutrons Quarks Superstring

Tiny loops of energy called superstrings are the most basic unit of matter and force in the universe, according to a theory of matter called string theory.

Bananas and all other objects in the universe consist of units called atoms. Atoms are made up of many smaller, subatomic particles. Protons and neutrons form an atom's *nucleus* (core), which is surrounded by electrons. Protons and neutrons are made of even smaller particles called quarks.

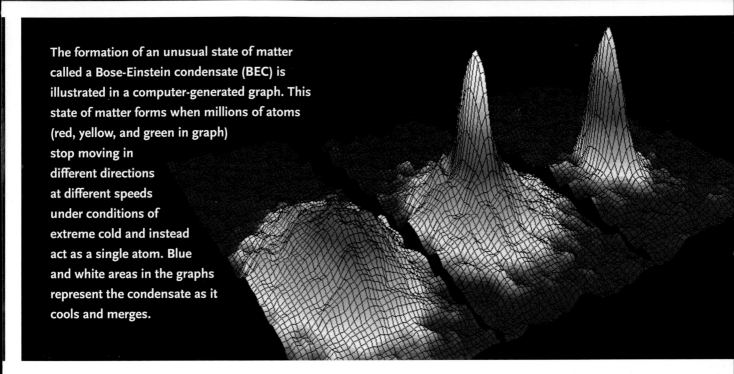

The formation of an unusual state of matter called a Bose-Einstein condensate (BEC) is illustrated in a computer-generated graph. This state of matter forms when millions of atoms (red, yellow, and green in graph) stop moving in different directions at different speeds under conditions of extreme cold and instead act as a single atom. Blue and white areas in the graphs represent the condensate as it cools and merges.

than 1.8 billion °F (1 billion °C). This was cool enough to allow protons and neutrons to join together to make objects that became the *nuclei* (centers) of atoms.

It took an additional 380,000 years for the temperature to cool down to about 5,400 °F (3,000 °C). The atomic nuclei could then attract and hold negatively charged particles called electrons. One or more electrons orbiting around a nucleus forms an atom. An atom is the smallest unit of a **chemical element.**

CHEMICAL ELEMENTS

Chemical elements are substances that contain only one kind of atom. The first element that formed was **hydrogen.** It is made up of one proton circled by one electron. The next element that formed was **helium.** Helium formed when hydrogen nuclei *fused* (joined) in the hot, dense universe. Great clouds of hydrogen and helium gas filled the early universe.

Stars and galaxies formed from the clouds of gas. In **nuclear fusion** reactions—the source of a star's power—atomic nuclei of one element fuse to form the nucleus of a different element. This reaction gives off tremendous energy. Nuclear fusion created other elements, including carbon, oxygen, and iron. As the cycle of star formation continued, more new elements formed. Scientists have discovered more than 110 chemical elements. Chemical elements form the molecules that make up all visible matter.

WHAT IS ANTIMATTER?

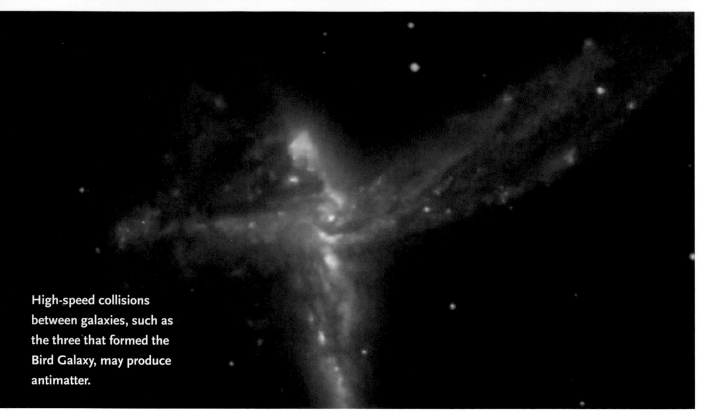

High-speed collisions
between galaxies, such as
the three that formed the
Bird Galaxy, may produce
antimatter.

ELEMENTARY ANTIPARTICLES

Scientists think that **antimatter** formed in the
first microseconds after the **big bang,** when
matter formed. Like matter, antimatter is made
up of particles. However, certain properties of
antimatter particles, such as their electric
charge, are the opposite of their matter "twins."

For example, an electron carries a negative
charge. Its antimatter twin, the positron, carries a
positive charge. The antiproton is the antimatter
opposite of the proton, and the antineutron is the
antimatter opposite of the neutron. An
antiproton, antineutron, and positron can join
together to create an antiatom.

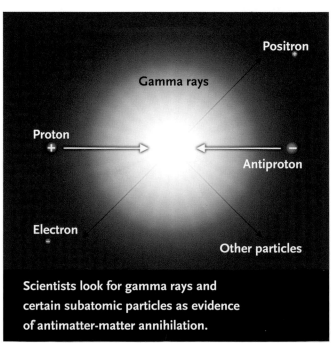

Scientists look for gamma rays and
certain subatomic particles as evidence
of antimatter-matter annihilation.

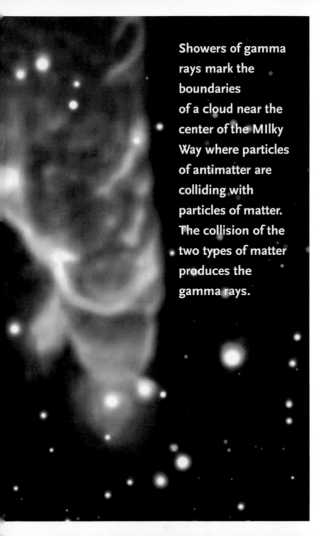

Showers of gamma rays mark the boundaries of a cloud near the center of the MIlky Way where particles of antimatter are colliding with particles of matter. The collision of the two types of matter produces the gamma rays.

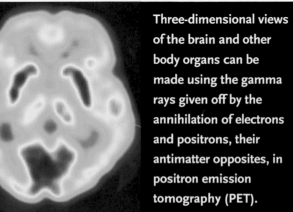

Three-dimensional views of the brain and other body organs can be made using the gamma rays given off by the annihilation of electrons and positrons, their antimatter opposites, in positron emission tomography (PET).

The most common way that scientists can study antimatter is in particle accelerators. These machines can boost the speed of electrons and other subatomic particles to almost the speed of light. The particles have as much energy as particles had in the early universe. By slamming the speeding particles into a gas, liquid, or solid target or an opposing beam of particles, scientists can produce enough energy to form antimatter. In 1995, physicists at the CERN lab in Switzerland created the first antiatoms in a particle accelerator. They made a small amount of antihydrogen.

MATTER VERSUS ANTIMATTER

When matter and antimatter meet, they destroy each other, leaving behind energy. However, in the first moments after the big bang, matter and antimatter were also created from energy. Energy, matter, and antimatter were continually being created and destroyed in the earliest microseconds after the big bang.

Today there is far more matter than antimatter. This situation presents a problem for scientists. If matter and antimatter were created in equal amounts right after the big bang, they should have totally annihilated each other. The universe would be filled only with energy. Something happened to give matter the edge over antimatter. Physicists calculated that it would have taken only one more particle of matter for every billion particles of matter or antimatter to create the matter-filled universe that we see today. A major question facing scientists is: Why was there more matter than antimatter to begin with?

WHAT IS ENERGY?

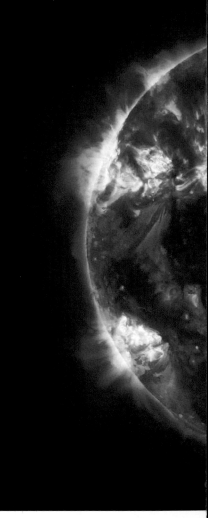

ENERGY TO MATTER

Today, four fundamental forces are responsible for all forms of energy. At the time of the **big bang,** there was only one force. In the first second after the big bang, the forces split off, creating four forms. These forces are the electromagnetic force; the strong nuclear force (responsible for holding an atomic *nucleus* (core) together); the weak nuclear force (involved in the breakdown of atoms); and **gravity** (the energy of attraction that matter has on other matter).

ENERGY IN THE ATOM

The great German-born American physicist Albert Einstein wrote a famous equation that showed how energy and matter can be exchanged. His equation, $E = mc^2$, means that energy is equal to matter times the speed of light squared.

Perhaps the most dramatic demonstration of how matter can be converted into energy involves the first atomic bombs, which the United States dropped on Hiroshima and Nagasaki in World War II (1939-1945). These weapons work by splitting atoms of either uranium or plutonium. The energy released drives a chain reaction that causes a tremendous explosion. Later, scientists learned how to create even more powerful hydrogen bombs that use **nuclear fusion** to create explosions. Scientists also learned how to generate electric power by splitting the atom in nuclear reactors.

A hydrogen bomb uses the *fusion* (combination) of hydrogen nuclei to produce tremendous amounts of energy. The same process happens in the core of a star.

Energy is the ability to do work. It takes one of four fundamental forms.

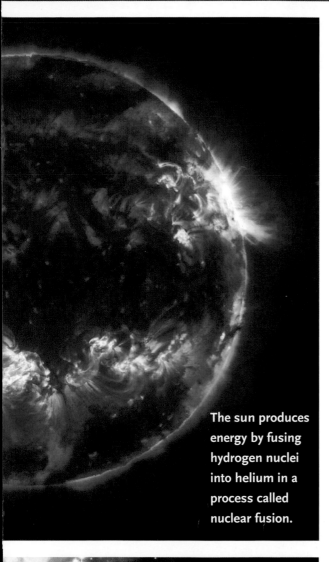

The sun produces energy by fusing hydrogen nuclei into helium in a process called nuclear fusion.

ENERGY FROM THE SUN

Nuclear fusion in the sun and other **stars** sends out **electromagnetic radiation** that makes these objects shine. Light from the sun is the source of almost all the energy on Earth. Plants use sunlight to create their own food. Animals get energy from eating plants. Ancient plant life died and decayed to form coal and oil. Much energy comes from burning coal and oil. In addition, differences in air temperature caused by heat from the sun creates wind. Engineers can capture the sun's energy directly to create electric power in solar cells or capture the energy in wind power using windmills.

Wind turbines tap into the energy in wind. That energy comes from differences in air temperature created by heat from the sun.

DID YOU KNOW?

Energy can be converted from one form to another. For example, our bodies change chemical energy in food to mechanical energy that we use when we move about.

FOCUS ON

USING PARTICLE ACCELERATORS TO STUDY THE EARLY UNIVERSE

The physical conditions of the universe immediately after the big bang were dramatically different from conditions today. The universe is far less dense and much cooler. The forms that matter takes are also far more complex. In order to study the simplest particles formed right after the big bang, scientists use particle accelerators. These complex machines produce the temperature, density, and the sheer energy of the universe's earliest moments. By colliding particles of matter at speeds approaching the speed of light, they can, for the briefest moment, re-create a time when exotic and strange particles existed.

The Large Hadron Collider (LHC) is the largest scientific experiment ever created. The underground accelerator tunnel (shown in outline) is about 17 miles (27 kilometers) in circumference.

The tunnel of the LHC contains many different types of particle detectors. More than 9,000 superconducting magnets are used to steer and focus two beams of light.

WHAT ARE MAGNETIC FIELDS?

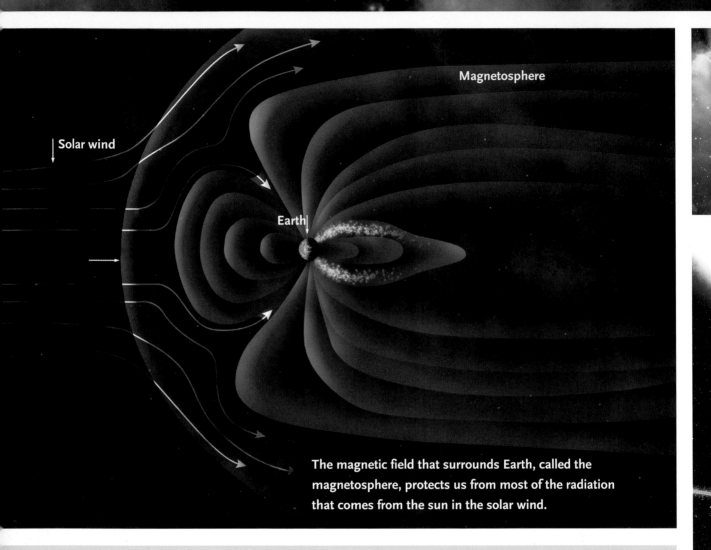

Magnetosphere

Solar wind

Earth

The magnetic field that surrounds Earth, called the magnetosphere, protects us from most of the radiation that comes from the sun in the solar wind.

SIMPLE MAGNETIC FIELD

Magnetism is related to electricity. Magnetism can be caused by the spinning movement of *electrons* (negatively charged particles) in certain atoms. Not all materials are attracted to magnetic fields. Magnets affect only certain metals, such as iron, nickel, and cobalt, and only these elements can become magnets.

The simplest magnetic field is one around a bar magnet. One end of the magnet is the north pole and the other is the south pole. Invisible magnetic field lines loop out of one pole and back to the magnet's other pole.

Magnets can attract or repel one another. The north end of one magnet will attract the south end of another. But the same poles of two magnets will repel each other.

Magnetic fields are lines of magnetic force around a magnet. The sun and other stars, Earth and some other planets, as well as entire galaxies are surrounded by magnetic fields.

A neutron star can produce powerful jets of energy from two opposite sides (thick white lines). It can also be extremely magnetic, producing powerful magnetic fields (thin blue lines). The star in this artist's depiction would probably be classified as a pulsar or a magnetar.

MAGNETIC FIELDS IN SPACE

Earth has a magnetic field. It is produced by the motion of currents in the liquid outer core. Earth's magnetic field protects the **planet** from the **solar wind** of the sun. The solar wind is a stream of electrically charged particles coming from the sun.

The sun is surrounded by a magnetic field. Eruptions of this field cause disturbances on the sun's surface. Huge prominences, loops of fiery gas, sometimes rise up from the sun's surface along a magnetic field. Sunspots—darker, cooler, areas on the surface of the sun—form from looping magnetic fields.

Other stars also have magnetic fields. Some are far more powerful than those of the sun. Collapsed stars called **neutron stars** have magnetic fields a thousand times as powerful as the sun's. Physicists measure magnetism with a unit called a gauss. The sun's magnetic field is 1 or 2 gauss. Some neutron stars have a magnetic field of 10 trillion gauss.

Astronomers have also detected magnetic fields in the Milky Way and other **galaxies.** They think that slowly rotating galaxies could have created these fields. They believe that such magnetic fields could affect the rate at which **stars** form.

WHAT ARE GALAXIES?

Two bright spots in the center of galaxy NGC 6240 mark the location of supermassive black holes. The black holes, surrounded by clouds of glowing, superheated gas, are only 3,000 light-years apart. Scientists believe they are spiraling toward each other and will eventually merge.

SIZE AND AGE

The universe contains hundreds of billions of **galaxies.** Galaxies come in many sizes. Astronomers estimate that the smallest galaxies contain as few as 100,000 **stars.** The largest galaxies might contain more than 10 trillion stars. At the center of most galaxies is a large **black hole.** A black hole is an object that is so dense, not even light can escape the pull of its **gravity.**

   Cosmologists believe that galaxies began to form about 500 million years after the **big bang.** Light from the oldest and most distant galaxy known traveled about 13 billion **light-years** to reach Earth.

KINDS OF GALAXIES

There are several kinds of galaxies. **Spiral galaxies** have the shape of pinwheels. They have arms that extend from the ends of a bar of stars in a central bulge. Most of the stars and gas are in the central bulge. The spiral

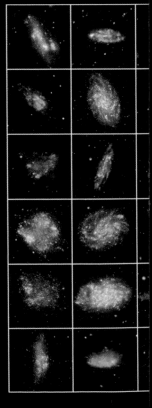

The age of a galaxy can be estimated by its color. Young stars tend to be relatively hot, making them appear bluer (left side of chart). Older stars tend to cool and shift toward a redder color (right side of chart).

and gas. They form the basic large-scale structures of the universe.

arms rotate around the center of the galaxy. The Milky Way is a barred spiral galaxy.

Galaxies with stars grouped in a ball shape are **elliptical galaxies.** Elliptical galaxies often contain more stars than gas. Astronomers believe that star formation used up most of the gas in elliptical galaxies.

Irregular galaxies come in a variety of shapes. Astronomers believe that some of these galaxies are very young. Other irregular galaxies may have formed when two galaxies collided. The gravity of a galaxy moving close by could have pulled another galaxy into an irregular shape. Irregular galaxies may contain more gas and dust than stars. For this reason, many new stars can form in irregular galaxies.

Peculiar galaxies are irregular galaxies with other odd features. Some are shaped like rings. Some are small and dim. Others have jets of matter shooting out from their centers. Still others have tails, perhaps caused by the gravitational pull of a nearby galaxy.

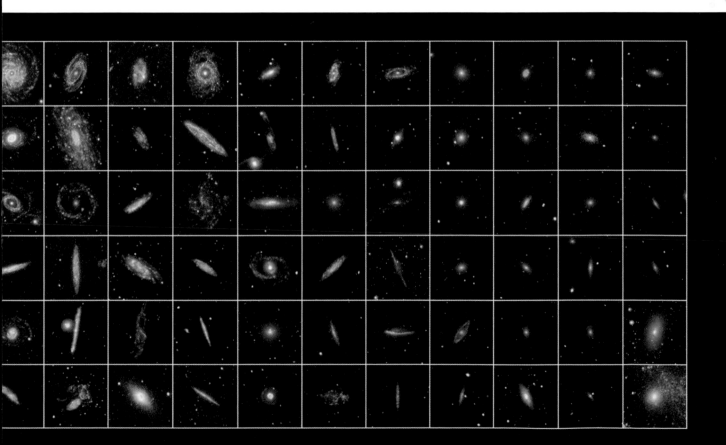

CLUSTERS OF GALAXIES

All **galaxies** belong to larger collections of these systems. The smallest collection of galaxies is called a **group.** The number of galaxies in a group may range from 20 to 100. The Milky Way, for example, belongs to the Local Group. This group contains some 40 galaxies and is about 10 million **light-years** wide. Groups contain galaxies of all sizes but usually have one or two large galaxies. The Milky Way and Andromeda are the largest galaxies in the Local Group.

A larger collection of galaxies is called a **cluster.** The Virgo Cluster is closest to the Milky Way. The Virgo Cluster contains about 2,500 galaxies. One of the densest known clusters is the Coma Cluster. It contains thousands of galaxies packed into a spherical shape more than 20 million light-years in diameter.

Clusters behave differently than individual galaxies. They contain a great deal of hot intergalactic gas. Unlike galaxies, clusters do not use up this gas by forming new **stars.** Instead, clusters hold onto it. Astronomers study the gas to determine when and how **chemical elements** formed from **nuclear fusion** reactions in stars in the cluster. They also want to understand how the elements traveled outward from stars inside the galaxies. Did **stellar winds** carry some of the chemical elements into intergalactic space? Did exploding stars blast some of the chemical elements out?

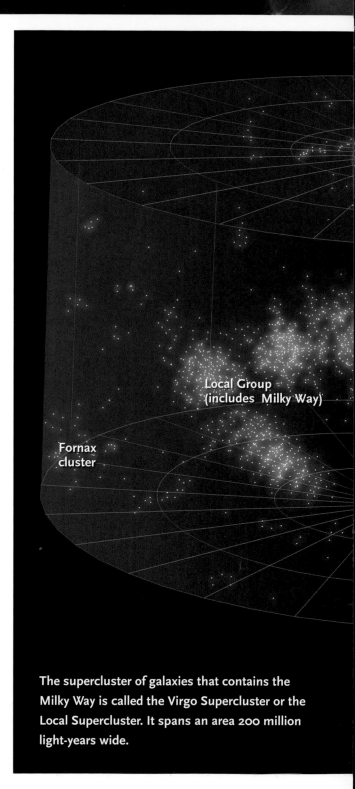

Local Group
(includes Milky Way)

Fornax cluster

The supercluster of galaxies that contains the Milky Way is called the Virgo Supercluster or the Local Supercluster. It spans an area 200 million light-years wide.

Clusters and superclusters are large groupings of galaxies that are held together by the force of gravity.

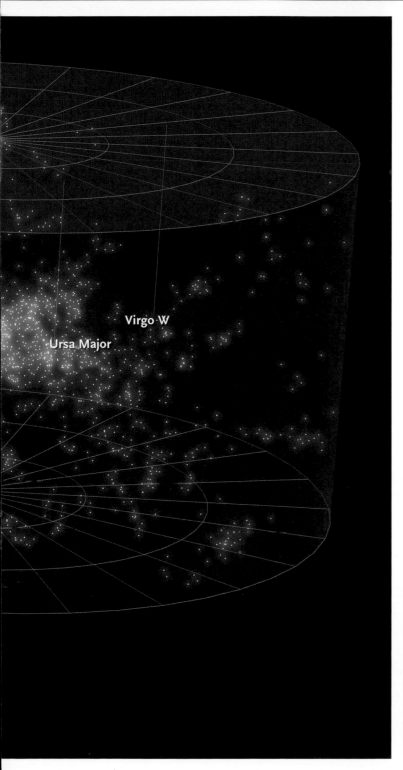

Virgo W

Ursa Major

SUPERCLUSTERS

Groups and clusters make up larger structures called **superclusters.** There are about 10 million superclusters in the universe that astronomers can see. The Local Group that contains our galaxy belongs to the Local Supercluster, which is also called the Virgo Supercluster. The Local Supercluster is made up of tens of thousands of galaxies. It is about 200 million light-years wide. Superclusters are gathered together into still larger structures that stretch across hundreds of millions of light-years.

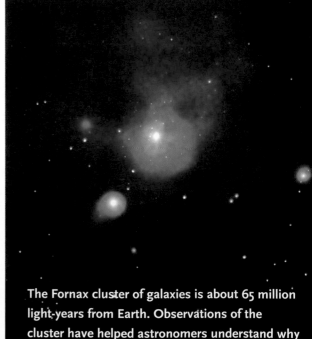

The Fornax cluster of galaxies is about 65 million light-years from Earth. Observations of the cluster have helped astronomers understand why clusters form where they do.

WHAT ARE FILAMENTS, WALLS, AND VOIDS?

LARGE-SCALE STRUCTURE

Astronomers have found that the universe is filled with large-scale structures. They discovered these structures from surveys of the sky. The surveys produced pie-shaped slices of the universe for astronomers to study. Some astronomers describe the universe revealed by these surveys as looking like a vessel filled with soap bubbles. These structures consist of huge networks of **galaxies** that form string-like filaments and immense walls. Vast regions of relatively empty space called voids surround the walls and filaments.

Two of the largest structures are called the Great Wall and the Sloan Great Wall. The Great Wall is a network of galaxies more than 500 million light-years long. The Sloan Great Wall is a region more than 1 billion light-years long. The Sloan Great Wall was discovered from data collected by the Sloan Digital Sky Survey. From 2000 to 2008, astronomers with this survey used a telescope at Apache Point Observatory in New Mexico to take pictures of about 25 percent of the sky, containing some 230 million objects.

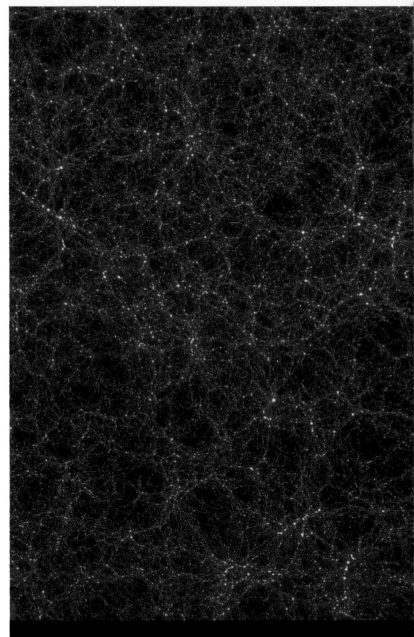

Galaxies appear as bright dots along filaments of matter (colorized in orange) in a computer-produced image of one section of the universe about 2.6 billion light-years across. The spaces between the filaments are filled with dark energy, a little-understood form of energy that apparently makes the universe expand more and more rapidly.

Filaments, walls, and voids are huge structures in deep space. Astronomers study these structures to learn about how matter and energy are distributed throughout the universe.

A CLUMPY UNIVERSE

Cosmologists and astronomers are trying to learn more about why matter is clumped into large-scale structures throughout the universe. They thought that after the **big bang,** the universe was almost perfectly smooth. Stars and galaxies would never have formed in a perfectly smooth universe.

The **cosmic microwave background (CMB) radiation** shows, however, that there were actually tiny variations in the distribution of matter and energy. Only 380,000 years after the big bang, these differences were enough to affect the CMB radiation. These tiny variations meant that some areas had stronger **gravity** than others. This gravity drew in additional matter, which eventually formed the first **stars** and galaxies. However, astronomers still have much to learn about how structures in the universe formed after the big bang.

The Milky Way lies on the border between an area of very little matter called a void (dark area) and a region dense with matter called the Great Attractor, as shown in a computer-generated image of the distribution of matter within about 300 million light-years of our galaxy.

Milky Way

Void

Great Attractor

Void

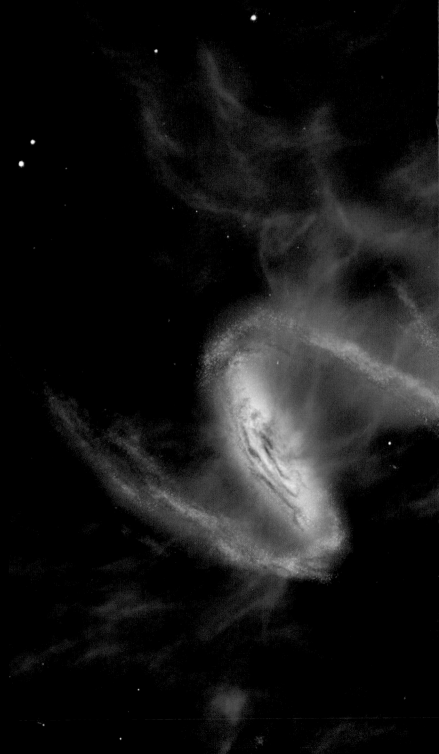

LYMAN-ALPHA BLOBS

Some of the most mysterious objects in the universe are gigantic, distant clouds called Lyman-alpha blobs. Blobs may be as large as 400,000 light-years in diameter, about four times the size of the Milky Way. The blobs discovered so far date from the first 2 billion years of the birth of the universe.

Blobs are named for the type of light they give off, called the Lyman-alpha line. The line appears in the extreme ultraviolet range of the spectrum. This light tells astronomers that the clouds are made almost entirely of hydrogen gas. Because stars and whole galaxies are made mostly of hydrogen, scientists are studying the blobs to see what role they may have played in the formation of the earliest galaxies.

Massive clouds of gas (orange) swirl ▶ around three galaxies (white) in the process of merging, in an artist's illustration of a Lyman-alpha blob. The galaxies, which are more than 11 billion light-years away, each shine with the light of more than 1 trillion suns. One theory suggests that the blobs are superwinds, eruptions of gas produced by the explosions of massive stars. Such stars result from periods of intense star formation triggered by the collision of galaxies.

A Lyman-alpha blob, as it looked 12 billion years ago (yellow), has what appears to be a supermassive black hole nearby (blue with red halo). The black hole may be the source of energy that lights up the surrounding blob of hydrogen gas. One theory about the blobs' origin suggests that they are the earliest clouds of matter that eventually condensed into the earliest galaxies.

GRAVITY AND MATTER

Gravity is one of the fundamental forces of nature. Gravity is a force that acts between objects that have *mass* (amount of matter). Gravity acts to pull matter together. Objects that contain more matter have stronger gravity. The intensity of gravity also depends on how close objects are to one another.

All objects attract each other. However, more massive objects have a greater influence on the motion of less massive objects. This attraction holds the less massive Earth and the other **planets** in orbit around the more massive sun. It holds the less massive moon in orbit around the more massive Earth.

Gravity also holds the sun and other **stars** together in our **galaxy,** the Milky Way.

Stars orbit around the center of galaxies. Astronomers have evidence that galaxies contain a supermassive **black hole** in the center. Black holes have such intense gravity that not even light can escape. Astronomers have determined that a supermassive black hole rests at the exact gravitational center of our galaxy. Based on its pull on surrounding stars, astronomers have concluded that the black hole contains as much matter as about 4 million suns.

GRAVITY AND STRUCTURE

Cosmologists believe that gravity played a role in helping shape the structure we see in the universe today. Although matter was originally spread out very smoothly, there

Even when merging galaxies are still far apart, gravity begins to create a bridge of dust and gas between them.

As the galaxies approach each other, their gravity pulls long tails of matter in swirls away from their cores.

These tails of matter become longer as the galaxies draw near and the pull of their gravity becomes more intense.

Gravity is the force that holds together galaxies, stars, planets, and moons in the universe. It also shapes the overall structure of the universe.

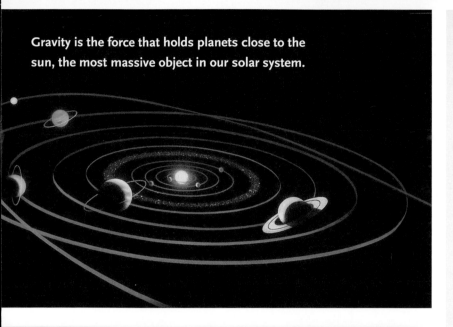

Gravity is the force that holds planets close to the sun, the most massive object in our solar system.

COSMIC COLLISIONS

The effects of gravity on colliding galaxies appear in six snapshots of galaxies at different stages of merging. It takes millions of years for galaxies to merge.

were places where there were slight variations. Cosmologists compare these differences to ripples in a pond. Gravity acted to pull more matter in toward the first concentrations of matter.

Gravity ultimately shaped the structure of the universe, pulling matter together to form **clusters** and **superclusters** of galaxies. However, scientists have discovered that the gravity of visible matter alone could not have formed the galaxies we see today. By studying the effects of gravity, scientists have determined that most matter in the universe is a mysterious, invisible substance called **dark matter.**

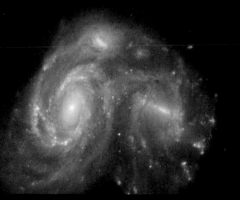

As the galaxies grow closer, massive, bright new stars form from colliding clumps of gas.

More and more matter falls in on the galaxies' cores, heating them until they glow with infrared radiation.

Finally, the cores of the galaxies merge, leaving long filaments of stars and gas extending from the new core.

WHAT IS THE FORCE OF GRAVITY?

The force of gravity, also known as gravitation, is the force of attraction that acts between all objects because of their mass. An object's mass is its amount of matter. German-born American physicist Albert Einstein discovered that gravity is actually a *warp* (bend) in the fabric of space itself. The more massive an object is, the more it bends surrounding space. Objects speed toward the center of these warps much as a marble rolls toward a bowling ball placed on a soft mattress. Einstein also discovered that space and time are bound together in an entity called space-time. One of the strange consequences of space-time is that time passes more slowly for a moving object than for an object at rest. As odd as they may seem, Einstein's revolutionary theories about gravity have been confirmed by a number of scientific experiments.

Less massive objects, such as stars ▶ the size of the sun, distort space-time less than more massive objects, such as neutron stars. The warp created by a black hole is so great that everything coming within a certain distance falls into it, never to escape.

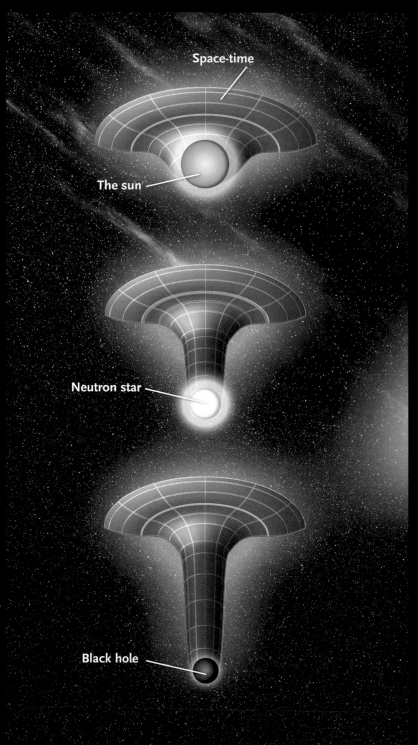

Space-time

The sun

Neutron star

Black hole

◀ Findings from Gravity Probe B, shown in an artist's illustration, have confirmed Einstein's prediction that a rotating body like Earth should slightly drag space-time around in the direction of its rotation.

Numerous monitors at a control center for the Laser Interferometer Gravitational-Wave Observatory (LIGO) project record data gathered by three detectors designed to measure disturbances in light beams caused by gravitational waves. Such waves, predicted by Einstein, are created by the collisions of stars or black holes and other movements of objects through space.

▼

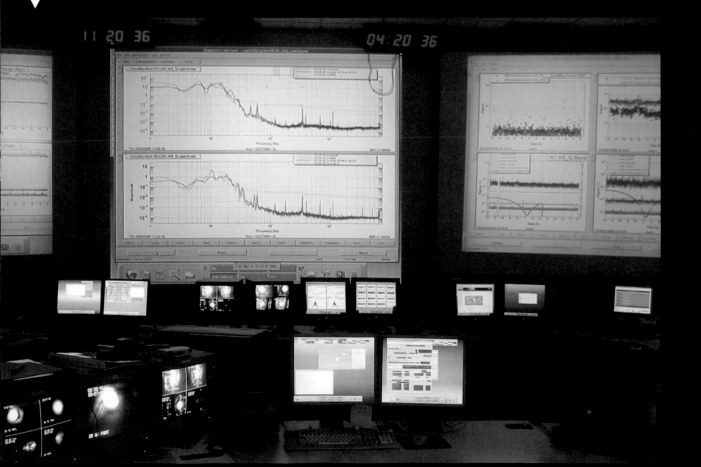

WHAT IS DARK MATTER?

HOW GALAXIES MOVE

Astronomers first began to suspect that most of the matter in the universe is invisible when Swiss astronomer Fritz Zwicky noticed that **galaxies** in the Coma Cluster were moving around each other at a surprising speed. The galaxies were moving too quickly to be held together by the **gravity** of their visible matter. In 1933, Zwicky suggested that the Coma Cluster must contain some kind of invisible matter. Gravity from this invisible matter held the cluster together. Over the years, scientists have found increasing evidence that there is far more invisible matter in the universe than visible matter.

LOOKING FOR ANSWERS

Scientists came to call the invisible matter **dark matter.** They are still exploring the nature of dark matter. Some scientists think dark matter is made up of electrically neutral, low-**mass** particles called axions. However, most physicists believe that dark matter is made up of **weakly interacting massive particles** (WIMP's). WIMP's are slow-moving particles that interact only weakly with other matter. Such particles could gather in the large, thin clouds of dark matter scientists believe surround galaxies.

Although scientists have not yet confirmed the existence of WIMP's, they have designed experiments to detect the mysterious particles. WIMP's rarely interact with matter, so they should

Clouds of dark matter (colorized in blue) surround a massive galaxy cluster (colorized in pink) that formed from the collision of two galaxy clusters, in a composite image made using data from the Hubble Space Telescope and Chandra X-ray Observatory. The collision slowed the visible matter in the clusters but not the surrounding dark matter.

DID YOU KNOW?

Unlike ordinary matter, dark matter does not give off, reflect, or absorb light rays. Scientists have detected dark matter through the effects of its gravitational pull on visible objects.

Dark matter is a mysterious, invisible form of matter that makes up about 85 percent of the matter in the universe.

pass through Earth. Most other particles are blocked by our **planet.** By building detectors deep underground, scientists hope to detect WIMP's without interference from other particles. Other scientists hope to find evidence of radiation given off by the few WIMP's that interact and annihilate each other. Still other scientists hope to create WIMP's in such particle accelerators as the Large Hadron Collider in Europe.

GRAVITATIONAL LENSING

A phenomenon called gravitational lensing provides evidence for the existence of dark matter. As light rays travel to Earth from a quasar, the gravitational effects of a galaxy in the rays' path act like a lens, causing the light rays to bend. As a result, the light rays gathered by a telescope on Earth seem to come from two images (inset, below left). When the gravitational lens is a cluster of galaxies (inset, below right), the light rays are bent even more, and the distant object appears as a ring of images (blue objects). The gravity of the cluster's visible matter is not sufficient to cause such lensing, indicating the presence of dark matter.

Quasar

Light rays

Galaxy

Double image of quasar

Telescope

Double image of quasar

Ring of multiple images of galaxy

WHAT IS DARK ENERGY?

Tycho's Supernova Remnant, which appeared in Earth's skies in 1572, was produced by a kind of supernova that astronomers use as a *standard candle* (object of known brightness) to measure the rate at which the universe is expanding.

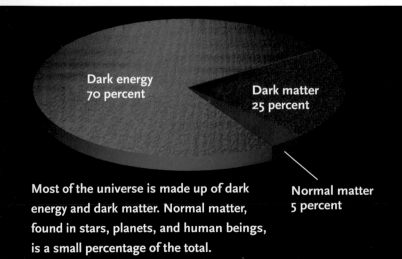

Dark energy
70 percent

Dark matter
25 percent

Normal matter
5 percent

Most of the universe is made up of dark energy and dark matter. Normal matter, found in stars, planets, and human beings, is a small percentage of the total.

CLUES FOR DARK ENERGY

In 1929, the American astronomer Edwin P. Hubble found that the universe is expanding. Scientists expected to find evidence that this expansion is gradually slowing, as **gravity** from matter in the universe acts against the expansion.

Scientists got a shock in 1998. Astronomers were studying images of very old and distant **supernovae,** or exploding **stars.** Certain supernovae all reach the same peak of intensity, which allows astronomers to use them as "standard candles." By measuring the *redshift* (shift of light to longer wavelengths) from such supernovae, astronomers found strong evidence that the expansion of the universe actually began to *accelerate* (speed up) about 5 billion years ago. Later studies of the **cosmic microwave background (CMB) radiation** and the large-scale structure of the universe confirmed these surprising results.

Scientists realized that an unknown source of energy was causing the accelerating expansion. They call this mysterious force **dark energy.** Remarkably, the rate of acceleration indicates that about 70 percent of the universe is made up of dark energy.

Dark energy is causing the expansion rate of the universe to speed up. Scientists know very little about what dark energy actually is.

HUBBLE WITNESSES A COSMIC TUG OF WAR

Dark energy and dark matter have worked against each other since the early universe, according to findings by the Hubble Space Telescope. Dark energy apparently makes the universe expand, while dark matter causes visible matter to come together. About 5 billion years ago, for reasons still unexplained, dark energy gained the upper hand over dark matter. As a result, the unverse has been expanding at an accelerated rate.

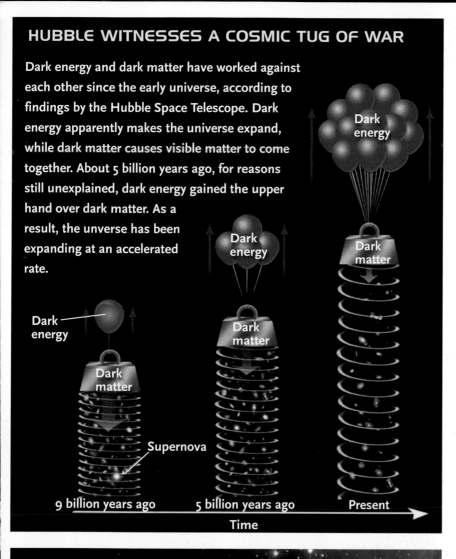

Dark energy

Dark matter

Supernova

Dark energy

Dark matter

Dark energy

Dark matter

9 billion years ago   5 billion years ago   Present

Time

DID YOU KNOW?

The expansion of the universe does not cause the matter within a particular object to expand. The attraction among its atoms and molecules holds the object together. The force of gravity prevents stars in a galaxy from moving away from one another. But galaxies move away from one another.

WHAT IS DARK ENERGY?

Scientists have named dark energy, but they know very little about what it actually is. Physicists have proposed a number of theories. One theory is that all of space is filled with energy called the cosmological constant. This constant has the same value everywhere. The constant presses outward in all directions, causing the expansion of space. As space expands, the total energy of the constant grows with it. Unfortunately, attempts to explain the cosmological constant mathematically have failed.

Another theory proposes that the acceleration is caused by an energy field called quintessence. Quintessence is similar to the cosmological constant, but its value changes over time and space.

Finally, some scientists suggest that the nature of **space-time** itself may change at very large scales. However, this theory contradicts Albert Einstein's theory of general relativity, which has been confirmed by many experiments.

EARLIEST SKY ORGANIZATION

It can be hard to tell one **star** from another when you look up at the sky. People in ancient civilizations, such as the Greeks and Romans, found a way to break up the sky into recognizable sections. They noticed that certain stars appeared to form imaginary patterns in the sky. The ancient Greeks named the imaginary patterns after mythical heroes, such as Orion, and heroines, such as Andromeda. Some **constellations** were named for animals, such as Leo, the lion, and Taurus, the bull. When European explorers sailed to the Southern Hemisphere from the 1400's to the 1700's, they picked out imaginary patterns in the stars and broke the southern sky into constellations also. The explorers named the constellations after scientific instruments and

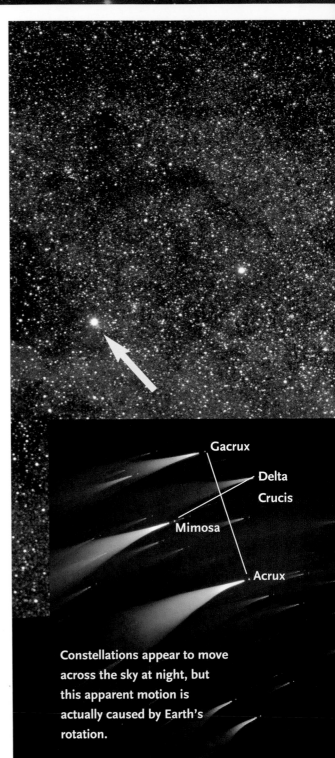

Gacrux

Delta
Crucis

Mimosa

Acrux

Constellations appear to move across the sky at night, but this apparent motion is actually caused by Earth's rotation.

Ursa Major, or the Great Bear, is one of the most familiar constellations. Some of its stars form the Big Dipper, though this group is not a true constellation.

A constellation is a group of stars in a region of the sky. There are 88 constellations in the night sky.

Gacrux

Delta Crucis

Mimosa

Acrux

The Southern Cross is easily visible in the Southern Hemisphere. The star nicknamed Mimosa points in the direction of Alpha Centauri, a bright yellowish star (arrow). Alpha Centauri is the nearest star system to Earth.

animals, such as Telescopium, for telescope, and Musca, for the fly.

Because of Earth's rotation, the constellations appear to move. The positions of the constellations in the sky also appear to change with the seasons. The apparent motion is caused by the Earth's tilt.

USING CONSTELLATIONS

Ancient peoples told many stories about the constellations, describing the struggles of heroes and gods. Because constellations appear to change position with the seasons, they also served ancient people as a kind of calendar, telling them when to plant crops.

Constellations are useful to astronomers and sailors for remembering the positions of individual stars. For example, Polaris, the North Star, is the last star in the handle of the Little Dipper, a ladle-shaped group of stars in the constellation Ursa Minor. Sailors once used Polaris to navigate the oceans of the Northern Hemisphere. Polaris is over the North Pole. By measuring how high Polaris was in the sky, navigators could calculate their latitude. Latitude shows how far an observer is north or south of the equator. Astronomers today use the names of stars and constellations to identify to other astronomers the positions of objects discussed in their research.

WHAT IS THE CELESTIAL SPHERE?

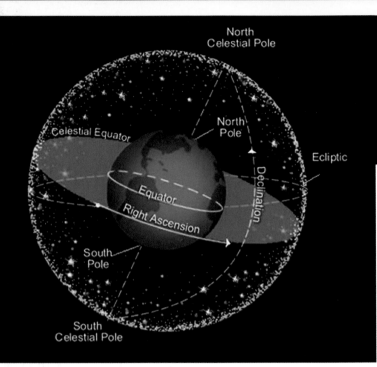

The celestial sphere is based on the ancient assumption that all stars are the same distance from the Earth. Today we know that stars vary tremendously in their distance. But the celestial sphere still provides a way to locate stars in the sky

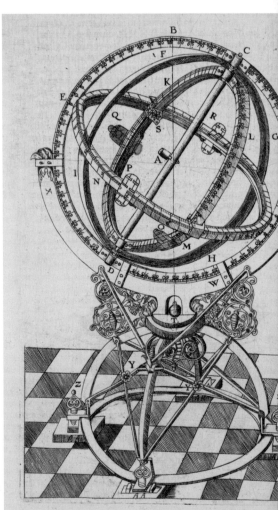

A celestial sphere designed by Tycho Brahe showing the sun and planets orbiting Earth is pictured in his book *Astronomiae Instauratae Mechanica*, published in 1598.

The ancient Greeks invented the system of celestial spheres. They believed the spheres were real. They thought that the heavens were made up of several spheres, one inside another. Some spheres carried the sun, moon, and **planets.** Other spheres carried the more distant **stars.** Today, we know that stars all occupy unique positions in space. However, the celestial sphere is still a useful tool.

PARTS OF THE CELESTIAL SPHERE

Earth is at the center of the celestial sphere. The north celestial pole and the south celestial pole are above Earth's north and south poles and extend outward into space. The celestial equator is a line around the celestial sphere directly above Earth's equator. The ecliptic is the imaginary path of the sun on the celestial sphere over the period of one day. The path of the sun changes by a little each day, so

The celestial sphere is an imaginary sphere that encloses the entire universe. It has been used since ancient times as a way of locating objects in the sky.

The Danish astronomer Tycho Brahe (1546-1601) was among the last astronomers who made observations using the unaided eye rather than a telescope. Several of the celestial spheres he used in his work are visible in this illustration from 1587.

the ecliptic moves from day to day during the year.

LOCATING OBJECTS IN SPACE

Astronomers use the celestial sphere to track objects in a sky that seems to move because of Earth's movements. Stars have "permanent" positions on this sphere. Astronomers use celestial coordinates to locate stars and other objects on the celestial sphere. The coordinates are called the right ascension and the declination. Just like the parts of the celestial sphere, the coordinates have counterparts on Earth. Right ascension is like latitude on Earth. Declination is like longitude on Earth.

DID YOU KNOW?

When viewed from Earth's Northern Hemisphere, stars rotate counterclockwise around the celestial north pole. Viewed from the Southern Hemisphere, stars rotate clockwise about the celestial south pole.

HOW DO ASTRONOMERS MAP THE UNIVERSE?

SKY SURVEYS

Astronomers have surveyed the sky since ancient times. By identifying patterns of **stars** and grouping them into **constellations** in the sky, the ancient astronomers made the first maps of the universe. Before the 1930's, astronomers plotted the locations of thousands of **galaxies.** These maps, however, were two-dimensional. They did not show how far a star was from Earth.

To create a three-dimensional map of the universe, astronomers point a telescope at an area of the sky for a long period. The longer a telescope looks at a region of sky, the more light it collects from distant objects. The first modern sky survey, the Palomar Observatory All Sky Survey, began in the late 1940's and lasted into the 1950's. The Palomar survey used an **optical** telescope that collected **visible light.** Later sky surveys used telescopes and satellites in space that collected different types of **electromagnetic radiation** from objects in space, including **radio waves, infrared light, ultraviolet light, X rays,** and **gamma rays.**

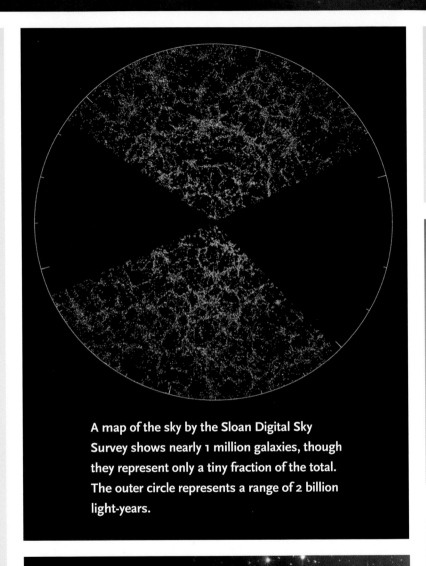

A map of the sky by the Sloan Digital Sky Survey shows nearly 1 million galaxies, though they represent only a tiny fraction of the total. The outer circle represents a range of 2 billion light-years.

DID YOU KNOW?

Some of today's constellations have their roots in patterns in the sky noted by the Sumerians in perhaps 2000 B.C. Chinese constellation patterns, which are largely different from those used in Europe, may also date from that time.

Astronomers use many tools to map the universe. Telescopic surveys of the sky and redshift surveys are the most valuable mapping tools.

REDSHIFT

The universe has been expanding for the last 13.7 billion years, ever since the **big bang.** The expansion stretches light waves as they travel through space. This stretching is called **redshift.** By measuring the redshift of light, scientists can estimate the distance the light has traveled. For example, light that left a galaxy 13 billion years ago shows strong redshift. It has been stretched so much by the expansion of space that it reaches the Earth as infrared or radio waves.

The radio telescope at Stanford University in California, called the Dish, is one of many used by astronomers to map the universe. The Dish measures 150 feet (45 meters) across and weighs about 300,000 pounds (136,000 kilograms).

3-D MAPS OF THE UNIVERSE

Astronomers once thought that stars were fixed on celestial spheres, but they know now that stars and galaxies occupy unique points in three-dimensional space. Scientists have only begun to map the hundreds of billions of galaxies that fill the observable universe, the part of the universe that we can see with our eyes and telescopes.

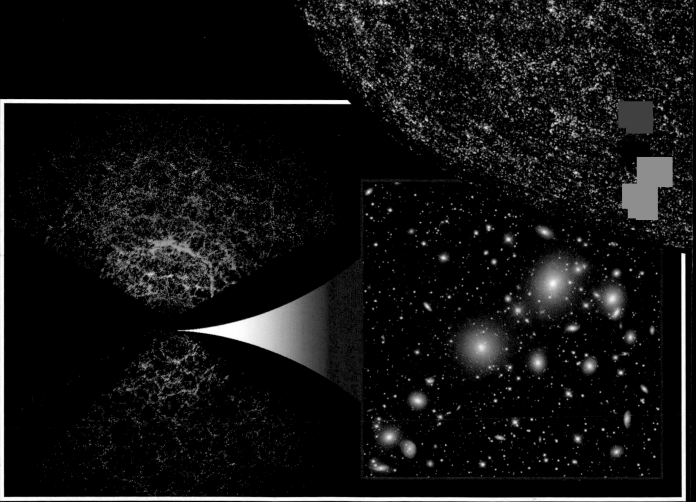

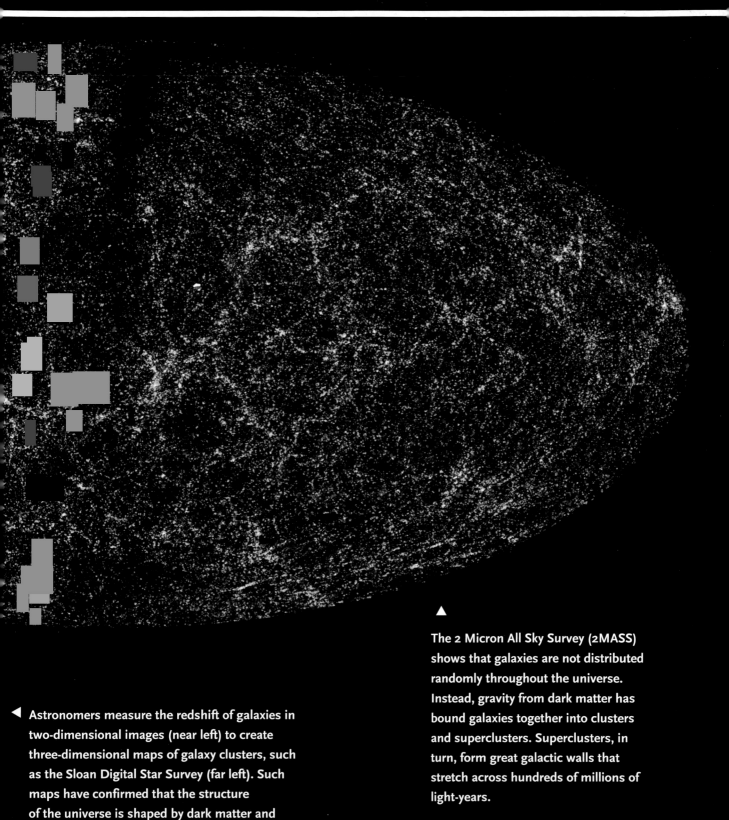

The 2 Micron All Sky Survey (2MASS) shows that galaxies are not distributed randomly throughout the universe. Instead, gravity from dark matter has bound galaxies together into clusters and superclusters. Superclusters, in turn, form great galactic walls that stretch across hundreds of millions of light-years.

◀ Astronomers measure the redshift of galaxies in two-dimensional images (near left) to create three-dimensional maps of galaxy clusters, such as the Sloan Digital Star Survey (far left). Such maps have confirmed that the structure of the universe is shaped by dark matter and dark energy.

MOVEMENT WITHIN GALAXIES

Individual **stars** as well as **galaxies** rotate. In the **solar system,** the **planets** orbit the sun. In turn, the sun orbits the center of the Milky Way, completing an orbit every 240 million years. The stars in both **spiral** and **elliptical galaxies** orbit their galactic cores.

MOVEMENTS OF GALAXIES

Within **galaxy groups** and **clusters,** galaxies orbit a common center of **gravity.** Within the Local Group that includes our galaxy, the two largest galaxies are the Milky Way and Andromeda. These galaxies are moving toward each other and will likely collide in a few billion years. Groups and clusters themselves move together through space. The Local Group is moving within the Local Supercluster, which contains about 100 groups and clusters. The **supercluster** itself also moves through space.

THE GREAT ATTRACTOR

Galaxies in our region of space are moving toward a huge concentration of matter called the Great Attractor at 1.4 million miles (2.2 million kilometers) per hour. Identifying the Great Attractor was difficult because it is hidden behind the center of the Milky Way. In fact, there may be more than one Great Attractor. The Milky Way and nearby galaxies are also being pulled by matter some 500 million light-years away. This distance is four times as far as the Great Attractor. The pull seems to come in part from

SPEED IS RELATIVE

- The solar system is orbiting the center of the Milky Way at 137 miles (220 kilometers) per second.

- Within the Local Group, Andromeda and the Milky Way are approaching each other at about 75 miles (120 kilometers) per second.

- Our Local Group of galaxies is moving toward the Great Attractor at about 375 miles (600 kilometers) per second.

Individual stars and galaxies move in relation to each other as the universe itself expands.

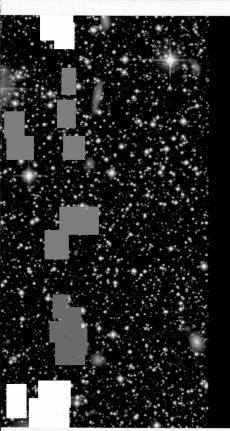

The Milky Way and all other galaxies within hundreds of millions of light-years are moving toward the Great Attractor. It is difficult to identify the Great Attractor because it is hidden by the disk of our galaxy. It may be an old, extremely massive supercluster that is part of an even larger structure.

the Shapely Supercluster. Even the Great Attractor is being pulled toward this supercluster.

EVERYTHING DIVERGES

All of the galaxies in the universe appear to be moving away from the Milky Way and from one another. This apparent movement is caused by the expansion of space itself. Picture the universe as a loaf of raisin bread. In the raw dough, the raisins are close together. As the bread bakes in the oven, the dough rises. Inside the dough, the raisins grow farther apart, but the raisins are not moving independently. In this way, galaxies are moving apart because the universe itself is growing larger.

- Galaxies in the Local Supercluster move at speeds of more than 930 miles (1,500 kilometers) per second in relation to the supercluster's center.

- The Local Supercluster is rushing through space at about 389 miles (626 kilometers) per second in relation to the cosmic microwave background (CMB) radiation.

THE HUBBLE CONSTANT

The Hubble Constant describes the apparent motion of distant galaxies, allowing scientists to measure the distance to galaxies by measuring their redshift.

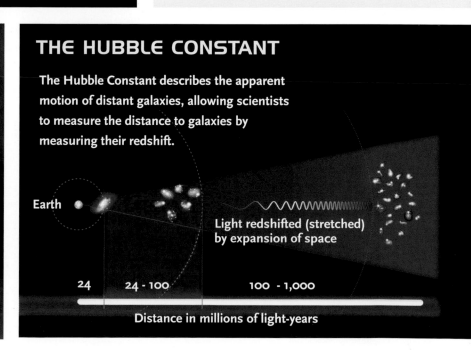

Earth

Light redshifted (stretched) by expansion of space

24   24 - 100   100 - 1,000

Distance in millions of light-years

STEADY STATE

Some scientists once thought it was possible for the universe to stay as it is forever. According to the steady-state theory, the universe had no beginning and would never end. Matter was constantly being created out of nothing to balance the expansion of space. The steady-state theory did not hold up, however. The discovery of distant **quasars** showed that the universe was very different in the past. The discovery of the **cosmic microwave background (CMB) radiation** was strong evidence that the universe began with the **big bang.**

THE BIG CRUNCH

Scientists also once believed that the force of **gravity** would stop the expansion of space. Eventually, space would contract, and all matter would come rushing back together in what cosmologists call the "big crunch." The big crunch could even lead to another big bang, and the universe would begin all over. However, the discovery that **dark energy** is causing the expansion of the universe to *accelerate* (grow faster) has caused most scientists to reject the idea of a big crunch.

THE BIG CHILL

If the universe does not come together in a big crunch, the **stars** will eventually use up their fuel and stop shining. The universe will grow cold and dark.

THE BIG RIP

Some cosmologists theorize that dark energy could lead to what they call the "big rip." In this scenario, dark energy would push the universe apart faster and faster. This rapid expansion could reverse the results of gravity. Galaxy clusters could come apart, and stars could be pulled out of galaxies. Finally, molecules and atoms could be split back into the subatomic particles that formed them. The universe as we know it would disappear into a thin haze.

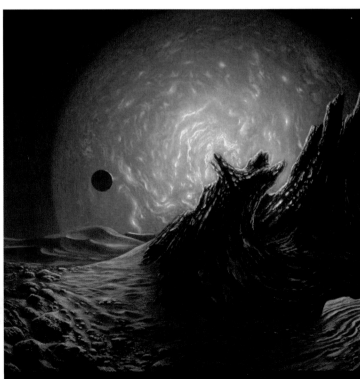

Long before the universe ends, the sun will become a red giant. It will grow so much larger that it may consume Earth. Fortunately, this event will not take place for another 5 billion years. The sun will burn out tens of billions of years before the universe meets its final fate.

THREE POSSIBLE FUTURES

Until scientists determine the nature of dark energy, the future of the universe will remain uncertain. Depending on the actual nature of dark energy, the universe has at least three possible—and very different—futures.

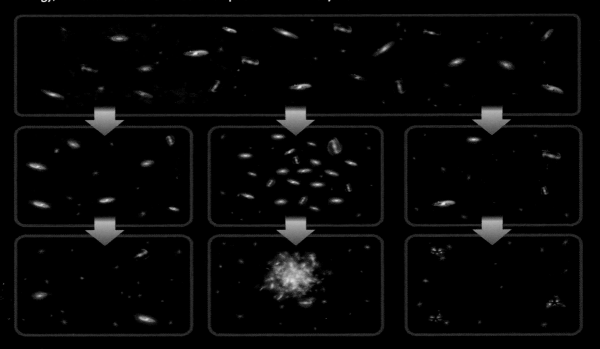

CONSTANT DARK ENERGY

If the density of dark energy remains the same (above), the expansion of the universe will accelerate at a constant rate, and galaxies will be pushed farther and farther apart. Within about 100 billion years, few other galaxies would be visible from our Milky Way.

BIG CRUNCH

If the density of dark energy decreases sufficiently (above), gravity will pull all galaxies back together in a "big crunch" within about 100 billion years. The universe could then experience another big bang.

BIG RIP

If the density of dark energy increases (above), the expansion of the universe will accelerate at an ever-increasing rate. Within about 50 billion years, every galaxy will be torn apart in a "big rip." According to this scenario, even atoms themselves will rip apart.

GLOSSARY

Antimatter – A substance that resembles ordinary matter but with certain properties of its particles, such as electric charge, reversed.

Big bang – The cosmic explosion that began the expansion of the universe.

Black hole – The collapsed core of a massive star. The gravity of a black hole is so strong that not even light can escape.

Chemical element – Any substance that contains only one kind of atom. Hydrogen and helium are both chemical elements.

Cluster – A concentration of hundreds to thousands of galaxies held together by gravity.

Constellation – A group of stars that resembles a familiar shape in the sky. Astronomers have divided the night sky into 88 constellations, such as Orion.

Cosmic microwave background (CMB) radiation – The most ancient electromagnetic radiation in the universe. Variations in the CMB radiation correspond to the distribution of galaxies in the universe today.

Cosmologist – A scientist who studies the structure and development of the universe.

Dark energy – A mysterious form of energy that is causing the expansion of the universe to accelerate.

Dark matter – A mysterious form of matter that does not reflect or absorb light. The majority of matter in the universe is dark matter.

Doppler effect – The change in wavelength of light or sound caused by the relative motion of the source and the observer.

Electromagnetic radiation – Any form of light, ranging from radio waves, to microwaves, to infrared light, to visible light, to ultraviolet light, to X rays, to gamma rays.

Elliptical galaxy – A galaxy with a shape that somewhat resembles a flattened globe.

Galaxy – A vast system of stars, gas, dust, and other matter held together in space by mutual gravitational attraction.

Galaxy group – A concentration of dozens of galaxies held together by gravity.

Gamma rays – The form of light with the shortest wavelengths. Gamma rays are invisible to the unaided eye.

Globular star cluster – A large group of stars held together by gravity. A globular cluster may contain tens of thousands to several million stars packed tightly together.

Gravity – The force of attraction that acts between all objects because of their mass.

Helium – The second simplest chemical element. Helium is produced through the nuclear fusion of hydrogen.

Hydrogen – The simplest chemical element. Hydrogen is the most abundant substance in the universe. It fuels most stars.

Inflation theory – The theory, in physics, that the early universe experienced an extremely brief period of particularly rapid expansion.

Infrared light – A form of light with long wavelengths. Also called heat radiation. Infrared is invisible to the unaided eye.

Irregular galaxy – A galaxy with a patchy, disorderly appearance.

Light-year – The distance light travels in a vacuum in one year. One light-year is equal to 5.88 trillion miles (9.46 trillion kilometers).

Mass – The amount of matter in an object.

Microwaves – A kind of radio waves with relatively short wavelengths. Microwaves are invisible to the unaided eye.

Neutron star – A star that has collapsed into a small area with extremely high mass. Neutron stars may form after massive stars explode.

Nuclear fusion – The combination of two or more atomic *nuclei* (cores) to form the nucleus of a heavier element. Nuclear fusion releases the energy that powers stars.

Optical – Of or relating to visible light.

Planet – A large, round heavenly body that orbits a star.

Quark – Elementary subatomic particles that make up the basic building blocks of matter.

Quasar – An extremely bright object at the center of some distant galaxies. Scientists believe quasars are powered by supermassive black holes.

Redshift – A shift in light's wavelength toward longer, redder wavelengths. Doppler redshift is caused by the Doppler effect. Cosmological redshift is caused by the expansion of the universe.

Radio waves – The form of light with the longest wavelengths. Radio waves are invisible to the unaided eye.

Solar system – The planetary system that includes the sun and Earth.

Solar wind – The continuous flow of particles given off by the outer atmosphere of the sun.

Space-time – Space conceived as a continuum of four dimensions, namely length, width, height, and time. Physicist Albert Einstein's theories of relativity showed that space and time are fundamentally joined.

Spectrum, spectra – Light divided into its different wavelengths. A spectrum may provide astronomers with information about a heavenly body's chemical composition, motion, and distance.

Spiral galaxy – A galaxy with a thin, disk-like structure and sweeping arms of stars wrapped about the galaxy's center.

Star – A huge, shining ball in space that produces a tremendous amount of visible light and other forms of energy.

Stellar wind – The continuous flow of particles given off by the outer atmosphere of a star.

Supercluster – A giant collection of galaxy groups and clusters containing tens of thousands of galaxies.

Supernova, supernovae – An exploding star that can become billions of times as bright as the sun before gradually fading from view. A supernova occurs when a massive star uses up all its fuel.

Ultraviolet light – A form of light with short wavelengths. Ultraviolet light is invisible to the unaided eye.

Visible light – The form of light human beings can see with their eyes.

Wavelength – The distance between successive crests, or peaks, of a wave.

Weakly interacting massive particle (WIMP) – A theoretical, slow-moving particle thought to make up dark matter.

X rays – A form of light with very short wavelengths. X rays are invisible to the unaided eye.

FOR MORE INFORMATION

WEB SITES

The Cosmic Distance Scale
http://heasarc.gsfc.nasa.gov/docs/cosmic
Zoom out from Earth to the planets and stars, distant galaxies, and beyond to understand how vast our universe is.

ESA Kids
http://www.esa.int/esaKIDSen
The European Space Agency's introduction to space science for kids.

Space Place
http://spaceplace.nasa.gov
NASA's Web site especially for students offers facts, games, animations, and projects about the universe.

StarChild: A Learning Center for Young Astronauts
http://starchild.gsfc.nasa.gov
A fun Web site from NASA that provides basic information about our solar system and the universe beyond, with suggestions for classroom activities.

Starry Skies Network
http://starryskies.net
Fascinating articles about the universe are arranged by such topics as archaeoastronomy, space tourism, space flight, and solar systems.

BOOKS

The Encyclopedia of Space and Astronomy
by Joseph A. Angelo and others (Facts on File, 2006)

George's Secret Key to the Universe
by Stephen and Lucy Hawking (Simon & Schuster Books for Young Readers, 2007)

The Handy Astronomy Answer Book
by Charles Liu (Visible Ink Press, 2008)

Planets, Stars, and Galaxies: A Visual Encyclopedia of Our Universe
by David A. Aguilar (National Geographic Society, 2007)

INDEX

ACKNOWLEDGMENTS

The publishers acknowledge the following sources for illustrations. Credits read from top to bottom, left to right, on their respective pages. All illustrations, maps, charts, and diagrams were prepared by the staff unless otherwise noted.

Cover: NASA, ESA, and The Hubble Heritage Team (STScI/AURA)

1   NASA/JPL-Caltech/R. Hurt (SSC)

4-5   NASA/ESA/N. Smith (U. California, Berkeley) et al./The Hubble Heritage Team (STScI/AURA)

6-7   NASA/B. Balick (U. Washington) et al./WFPC2/HST; NASA/JPL; NASA/JPL-Caltech; NASA/JPL-Caltech

8-9   Richard Powell; WORLD BOOK illustration by Matt Carrington; NASA

10-11   WORLD BOOK illustration; © D. Parker, Photo Researchers; NASA/ESA/The Hubble SM4 ERO Team; WORLD BOOK illustration by Matt Carrington

12-13   WORLD BOOK illustration by Ernest Norcia; WORLD BOOK illustration by Matt Carrington

14-15   WORLD BOOK illustration by Matt Carrington; WORLD BOOK illustration by Matt Carrington; WORLD BOOK illustration by Luke Haddock

16-17   Hubble Heritage Team (AURA/STScI/NASA); NASA

18-19   WORLD BOOK illustration by Matt Carrington; NASA, K. Lanzetta (SUNY)/Adolf Schaller (STScI); WORLD BOOK illustration by Matt Carrington

20-21   NASA/WMAP Science Team; ESA, LFI & HFI Consortia (Planck)/Axel Mellinger

22-23   NASA/TRACE; WORLD BOOK illustration by Luke Haddock; NIST/JILA/CU-Boulder

24-25   European Southern Observatory; NASA/CXC/M. Weiss; NASA/JPL-Caltech/J. Bally (Univ. of Colo.); Jens Langner

26-27   Department of Defense; NASA/TRACE Project, Stanford-Lockheed Institute for Space Research/Michael Benson, Kinetikon Pictures; © Brian A. Jackson, Shutterstock

28-29   © CERN

30-31   NASA/CXC/M. Weiss; WORLD BOOK illustration by Matt Carrington

32-33   NASA/CXC/MIT/C. Canizares, M. Nowack/STScI; NASA

34-35   © Andrew Zachary Colvin; NASA/CXC/Columbia U./C. Scharf et al.

36-37   © James Wadsley, McMaster University, Hamilton, Ontario; European Southern Observatory

38-39   NASA/JPL-Caltech/R. Hurt (SSC); NASA/ESA/CXC/JPL-Caltech/STScI/NAOJ/J. E. Geach (Univ. Durham) et al.

40-41   NASA/ESA/The Hubble Heritage Team (STScI/AURA)-ESA/Hubble Collaboration and A. Evans (University of Virginia, Charlottesville/NRAO/Stony Brook University)/K. Noll (STScI)/J. Westphal (Caltech); WORLD BOOK illustration by Rob Wood

42-43   WORLD BOOK illustration by Matt Carrington; NASA; Tobin Fricke, LIGO

44-45   NASA/CXC/CfA/M. Markevitch et al./ESO WFI/Magellan/U. Arizona/D. Clowe et al.; NASA/J. Bahcall; WORLD BOOK illustration; NASA/W. N. Colley and E. Turner, Princeton University/J. A. Tyson, Bell Labs, Lucent Technologies

46-47   NASA/CXC/SAO/JPL-Caltech/MPIA, Calar Alto, O. Krause et al.; NASA; NASA/ESA/A. Field

48-49   © Ian Ridpath; European Southern Observatory; © Stefan Seip

50-51   NASA/Lunar and Planetary Institute; © SSPL/Getty Images; Granger Collection

52-53   © M. Blanton/SDSS; Steve Jurvetson

54-55   Max Tegmark/Sloan Digital Sky Survey; NASA/JPL/Two Micron All-Sky Survey

56-57   European Southern Observatory; NASA, ESA, and A. Feild (STScI)

58-59   © Don Dixon; WORLD BOOK illustration by Paul Perreault